Trading Video Games

Make it Your Business

By Dave Morgan

Beginners' Guide for Professionally Trading Wholesale Video Games

Table of Content

Introduction 3
Chapter 1. How to Make Business Trading Video Games 5
Chapter 2. How to Buy from Wholesalers 13
Chapter 3. Buying from Wholesalers – Prices that You will Get 19
Chapter 4. New Releases vs. Back Catalogue Games 28
Chapter 5. Selling Video Games to Wholesalers and Retailers 36
Chapter 6. What are Game Codes, CD Keys, Digital Distribution 53
Chapter 7. Dropshipping 56
Chapter 8. Trading with Amazon 64

Introduction

The book describes how to make business trading video games. It is intended for both beginners, who have started trading recently or those who are just thinking of setting up their business of buying and selling PC and video games. The book will also be useful for those who have been already trading for some time and would like to develop their skills further.

Not only business owners but also employees of video game trading companies, such as buyers and the sales personnel will benefit from the book.

Chapter 1 gives general idea what it is to trade games in today's world and how to compete with others. Chapter 2 addresses specifics of how to source your product and buy it from wholesalers. Chapter 3 provides insight on how wholesalers price their products. Chapter 4 analyses specifics of trading new releases of video games vs. back catalog items. Chapter 5 provides details on how to sell video games to other game companies, wholesalers and retailers. Chapter 6 gives an idea on what's game codes in digital distribution, and

Chapter 7 describes what's dropshipping. Finally Chapter 8 provides information on how to trade with Amazon.

While you are reading the book, it would be beneficial to register on WholesGame in order to get a comprehensive list of wholesale video game suppliers.

Chapter 1. How to Make Business Trading Video Games

The book describes how to buy video games and PC games from wholesalers and sell to your customers. Trading video games can be quite profitable. There is a wide range of businesses involved in this, from tiny online stores to large national retail chains. The entry is relatively easy and does not require much initial investment. Many have started by trading on Ebay, or by opening a shop on Amazon, or launching a simple website of their own. Many have not grown further, but there are some who managed to increase their trade and become successful businesses.

Who can Trade Games

Because of easy entry, the industry of trading video games is very competitive. There is a large number of individuals and companies who at some time try to enter this niche. Many people, who like playing video games, assume that trading them would be as easy and as much fun as playing them. This is a common misconception, in reality trading video games is a hard job, and it requires certain skills and knowledge, like trading any other products. Luckily, good knowledge of video games, i.e. product knowledge, does help significantly. There is over 10,000 titles of video games available in the market, of which, around 3,000 titles are actively traded at any point of time, and good knowledge of games and their specifics, helps to sell them better.

Good product knowledge is not enough though, in order to be successful, one also needs skills and knowledge in marketing, sales, buying, and at least basics of accounting and finance.

Buying Games

One of the ingredients to successful trade is to have good suppliers, who can offer a wide range of products for good prices. Wholesale business is quite saturated and competitive, there is a wide range of suppliers in the market, including brick and mortar traditional wholesalers with their own warehouses, and virtual dealers who do not keep stock. This later are intermediates between stock keeping wholesalers and buyers.

There are many specifics and nuances on how to approach potential suppliers, how to establish good trade relationship and obtain good prices. In later chapters it is described in greater details how to work with suppliers. For now, in a nutshell, the necessary steps include: 1) researching and finding a list of potential suppliers; 2) preparing a brief introduction of your company and a request for stock list and prices; 3) assessing the stock lists from those who have responded, requesting application forms for opening accounts; 4) requesting a credit limit and negotiating a better price band if available.

Stock or not Stock?

There are two considerably different approaches on stocking the goods. Traders who do not stock the goods tend to buy stock after they have already pre-sold it to their customers. This allows to save on storing costs and, in a way, guarantees the sale. Major drawback is that there is a risk, after pre-selling an item, not to be able to buy it in a reasonable time because the item might be sold out at your suppliers. Such traders try to have as many suppliers as possible to overcome this issue, which makes them sporadic and irregular buyers, and suppliers tend to appreciate them less as customers.

More traditional way is to first buy and store items and then sell them. Such buyers have a steady flow of orders to their suppliers, they are appreciated as being better buyers, and manage to get better prices from suppliers. Such traders are also more reliable for supplying their customers because they sell what they already have in stock.

Selling Games

There is a number of places where traders can sell the games for commercial gain. One of the most common and easy places to start is Ebay. Traders can open free accounts, take orders, accept payments by PayPal or credit cards. Buyers have possibility to rate traders and leave reviews about their service. Based on buyers feedback, traders gain scores, which indicate both the number of people who provided the scores and the percentage of buyers who thought their service was good. A high score on Ebay, especially gained from a large number of customers, is a good asset, it is the trader's reputation, which can be capitalized by providing its owner an increased sales.

Another sales platform is Amazon. This is a paid service for traders. They need to pay monthly fees to keep their store on Amazon. In addition Amazon would collect commission on every transaction, plus there will be additional fees if trader chooses to use Amazon's Fulfilment Service. A more detailed description on how to trade on Amazon is in later chapters.

Many traders would launch their own website, usually an e-commerce store (e-store) to sell their products. E-commerce websites can be ordered from web developers, or web-literate traders may choose to develop their own web store themselves. There are many software packages in the market that allow to do this with relatively modest knowledge in web programming. Some of these packages are free, such as for example Presta Shop or Opencart, which are quite good e-store CMS software, though their free versions are quite basic, and most of the e-stores would also require additional features, called add-ons, which are not free and are sold for a price.

There are also paid software packaged and services that offer even more advanced features. For examples Shopify is a monthly subscription service that allows to build professionally looking online stores for your business.

Any e-store needs to be promoted in order to attract customers, including SEO for getting better positions in Google's search results, or/and advertisement on Google's AdWords for getting pay-per-click visitors.

With an increasing competition it is generally getting more difficult and more expensive to promote e-stores. There are only 10 results on the first page of a search engine, and there are thousands of stores who compete for appearing on that first page. Your site has to compete with Amazon, Game, Gamestop, and other Internet monsters, as people tend to buy mostly from sites that occupy the top three to five results on the search results page. Websites that are not on the first page are missing up to 90% of visitors, and have very small potential for selling. Plus, information websites, such as Wikipedia, IGN, Gamespot and few others may usually take couple of top places on the first page with an informational description of the product, which leaves even less available space on the first page.

Traditional brick and mortar stores also get significant competition nowadays. Even large retail chains such as Game, Gamestop, Best Buy, and Comet, are facing tough times. Some traders can take advantage of opening a local video game store for a local community, but with increasing reach of online giants such as Amazon, it is getting increasingly hard for traditional shops to compete.

Find a Niche

The best strategy, especially for a small trader, is finding a relevant niche, where he/she can be competitive. This can be either a specific range of games, or supplying a specific geographic region, or, especially in online sales, supplying some specific social groups. An e-store has a much more selling potential if it is connected with a successful online resource, for example a successful blog, or a web forum, or an information website that already has significant audience.

The role of social media sites, such as Facebook, Instagram, Twitter, Reddit, and others are becoming increasingly important in online marketing. A successful relevant social group on Facebook or a group of followers on Twitter may create significant number of potential customers and leads. Both Facebook and Twitter allow segmentation of audience hence giving opportunity to serve a relevant niche.

It is very difficult to compete on mass products with the giants, they would most probably provide a better price, and a wider distribution. It is always possible though to find a niche that they have missed. Clever trading is avoiding tough competition by finding opportunities that larger and stronger competitors have missed, and using them. This allows sailing into more quiet waters of niche competition rather than struggling in storms created by large players.

Selling video games is a difficult business nowadays, but it is also interesting and fun. A creative entrepreneur has a lot of opportunities using good knowledge and skills to build a successful business, compete in the marketplace, and grow.

Chapter 2. How to Buy from Wholesalers

Introduction

How to trade with large companies?
Many traders target large companies as their potential suppliers or even customers, and hoping to get significant profits from such trade. It may be possible though there is a significant number of challenges and considerations on the way. We will go through some of these challenges and will highlight some problems from the other side, i.e. from the side of a distributor. We will indicate some most common mistakes and problems encountered by applicants, so that you are better equipped when you approach a large company in your industry next time.

As a general rule, it is good to have access to more than one supplier. This allows to have both a wider variety of products at any given time and better prices. Even if you already have an account with, what you believe, is the best supplier in your region, it makes sense to constantly monitor the market for other suppliers and always have a choice of them. In practice, as a trader you constantly look for other companies, not only for new potential customers but for new potential suppliers. Sometimes they may overlap. Search for companies is a constant permanent process, and for good traders it is very important to develop efficient technics for finding and researching companies.

Finding Them

First of all how to find them? Well, there is a number of obvious options in every territory, companies that everybody know about, such as Gem, Koch, CentreSoft in the UK, for example. There are many other distributors and wholesalers, and it is worth approaching them too. Internet is obviously the main source for searching companies today. Many of the companies would have websites where you can get the first hand information about them.

Amazingly, many of these large companies would have very simple, unattractive websites, which lack any high tech sophistication and proper design. It is surprising to see how little attention many of the wholesalers and distributors may pay to their presence in the Internet. It is getting difficult to judge how good a company is nowadays, only based on their website. It is easy to build a fancy website and many, even very small traders may afford quite good looking professional websites, in opposite to some of these large companies who still use their websites, designed probably by the then CEO's student cousin back in 1993.

In addition to company's website, there are many other resources that can provide valuable information about the company, such as [WholesGame database](), industry and sector associations, the company house database, yellow pages and company directories, and many other online resources. There are also many specific discussion forums in the Internet, with members who are small and medium size traders, like you, who share their experience and opinion in dealing with specific wholesalers and distributors. Recently the social networking sites, especially LinkedIn have become very good for getting additional information about companies.

There is a wealth of information in the Internet. In many cases, you can do a cross-check, i.e. compare information about the same company from different sources. Significant discrepancies should be alarming.

Unfortunately there are many companies or individuals in this particular industry who would like to pretend larger and more significant than they really are. Contacting and dealing with such traders would be a waste of time in the best case. In worse case, there are many fraudsters out there too. It is a good idea to do a proper research and some diligence before contacting potential suppliers.

Contacting Them

Once you short listed companies that you would be willing to use as suppliers, it is time to contact them. Most of them would have a sales e-mail address for contacting them. Frist impression is very important, and a well written professional message is paramount for making that good impression. Your message should include at least the following components: greeting; the objective, i.e. opening account and receiving the stock list and prices; and brief information about your company.

The latest is the most important, because large companies may receive dozens of e-mails with requests every day, and messages from applicants that do not bother to properly introduce themselves have way less chances to be given proper attention and responded. An e-mail message from a hotmail account, which would only say "hi i was wandering if i can open account with yourselves, thanks." could be quite irritating. The information about you should ideally include your name, the name and address of your company, phone numbers, type of your company, are you an online trader, a brick and mortar retailer, or wholesaler, which countries do you trade in, how many outlets do you have, and an approximate estimation of product – games and console that you would buy per month.

If you can provide this information in your first message, it will quite positively make you different from many other messages that they have received that day. A very good idea is to have an e-mail signature with your company's name, address, phone, website, etc., it looks more professional.

Keep it short though, a message with multiple pages would not make a reader happy, and leaves less chances that it would be read at all.

Application

Once they find you suitable, most of the large distributors and wholesalers would require filling in their application form for setting up an account. If they are satisfied with your initial request, they will e-mail you their application form. Some of them may require submission of some other documents in addition to filling in their application form, such as for example your company registration certificate, your VAT registration certificate, a letter of introduction, etc. You will need to fill in the application form, sign, and send it back to them. At that point you may be assigned an account manager at their company, who will be dealing with you. It may take several days before they set up an account, and finally, oh miracle! you will receive an e-mail informing that your account has been set up.

What happens next will be described in our next Chapter.

Chapter 3. Buying from Wholesalers – Prices that You will Get

In previous Chapter we have discussed how to find wholesalers and distributors of video games, consoles, and consumer electronics, and how to apply for an account with them. Suppose you were successful and have received a response from a distributor that they had opened an account for you. Very good. Next step, they will give you an access to their stock list with prices. Here, it starts to get a little complicated.

Supplier or Broker?

First of all, we will need to find out whether the items in stock list are actually physically present in a distributor's stock or not. There is a difference if distributor sells goods that it does or does not have in stock. Those that do not, so called brokers, after receiving your order, will get on the phone and start searching where they can get the required stock for you, and it is not quite certain when they will be able to find it, in what condition they will find it, and if they will find anything at all. Some wholesalers that sell in such manner, can offer lower price, since they have lower costs because they do not need to own or rent a warehouse, do logistics, etc. Though this is not necessarily the case because due to relatively small orders from their suppliers, they do not get the best prices and their cost may be high anyway. In other words, this is not really a best option.

Such suppliers could be used occasionally, as a backup option, if a certain item cannot be found anywhere else, but not permanently because it most probably mean extra costs, longer waiting time, and hassle. It is better to deal with wholesalers that have a warehouse where they keep their stock. They sell what they have in stock. As soon as they receive an order, and payment, they can ship out. In certain cases, such suppliers may sell stock that they do not have yet, for example items that haven't been released yet through pre-orders, or items through back orders if the supplier is confident that it will receive the stock in certain time period.

Wholesale vs. Retail Price

The second thing that will definitely create questions is the prices that you get. And here where it gets really confusing. It seemed that everything was going well so far, we found a good supplier, managed to open an account with them, now we are going to get their low prices, buy lots of goods and earn lots of money by reselling, isn't that great! Not exactly. Unfortunately it is unlikely that we will get good prices from them. At least not in the beginning.

But first of all let us clarify what is a good price? Good example is large retailers, such as Game, Play, and of course Amazon. They have everything, all kinds of products, very nice websites, product descriptions, pictures, and prices. Since these are retailers, it is natural to expect that we would be offered prices that should be lower than the prices at these stores. Of course, how else we can make a profit? Not exactly I am afraid. After receiving a stock list from our wholesaler, we may discover that many of the prices in the stock list are actually MORE expensive compared with the prices of some retailers. What is wrong? There are two explanations here.

First of all there is no wholesaler or distributor that can offer the lowest prices on ALL of its stock items. Large distributors have thousands of items in stock. Some items have low prices, other items not so low, there are also some items that are definitely quite expensive. The price of an item depends on many factors, such as the cost that the wholesaler has paid to purchase the item, how many it has available in stock now, how quickly the wholesaler would be willing to spare that stock, what the competition for that item is, who else sells it, and for how much, as well as about a hundred of other factors.

And this is not all either. It appears, comparing with the prices of Game, Amazon does not really make much sense, because their prices and the driving forces that influence those prices are in quite different dimension. Let me give you a simple example. Many large retail chains sell video game consoles below the cost. Why do they do it? Because they earn their margins on selling video games. They have calculated that even though they will lose on sale of consoles, as a result they will earn more on selling the games. They are large and they can afford making loss in one product in order to make more profit in another. They are so big that they actually drive the prices. The huge retail chains purchase in tens of thousands units directly from the manufacturers with huge discounts for super low prices, and then they sell these consoles with even lower prices!

Think what are the chances of other resellers, including wholesalers, to sell these consoles even cheaper? Chances are none. The large retailers can offer the consoles cheaper anyway. And you or your suppliers cannot even buy from these retailers, not the wholesales quantities that you need. They sell only few pieces per person. This is understandable because the product is subsidized by them.

As a result, for such items one can observe a price paradox, when wholesale prices could be more expensive than retail price! This becomes a frequent cause of misunderstanding between a buyer and a new supplier, because the buyer gets an impression that the new supplier is trying to rip them off and impose some unreasonable prices. It is not really the case, the wholesaler itself may appear to have higher purchase prices that some large retailers prices.

Price Banding

There is something else that we need to know about the prices. It appears wholesalers and distributors have different price bands for different customers. Yes, that's right. Different price levels for different customer, and the prices may be considerably different. The most expensive prices are usually offered to customers, who the distributors do not want to deal with, and would like to get rid of. The lowest prices are for large and most loyal customers, such as other distributors and wholesalers, especially in countries that have low market prices.

Depending on what information a distributor gets from you during your application process, plus the information that the distributors finds on you for other sources, they would offer you a relevant price band. They are unlikely to inform you which band they have assigned to you, but if do ask them, they might inform you how many price bands they have and which particular band you have received. You may ask them what needs to be done for getting a better price band. It most probably would be connected with the volumes of buying. It would be wise not to rush into committing volumes that you would not be able to fulfil. Work it out slowly and eventually. You may request discounts on specific orders. You may be in not a favourable price band but you can always ask for a discount on a good order.

This is tricky though. If you buy hundred different items, one piece of each, it is unlikely that you will get any discount on such an order. But if you buy hundred pieces of one item, you can definitely ask for a discount and you will most probably get one. If you periodicity do such orders, you may soon request to move you to a better price band. How much better? Well, a £0.2 – £0.3 discount on a game is a good discount, a £1.00 – £1.50 on a console is also a very good discount. More is needed? For that, you will have to make an order for thousands of games or hundreds of consoles. We need to understand that distributors and wholesalers usually work with small margins, they earn on large volumes, and there is no much room for making a considerable discount, and we should be realistic in how much discounts we can expect.

Using What We Have

Let's try to draw some conclusions. First of all, we should not get upset if we have initially received prices from a distributor that turned out to be much higher than we were expecting. We saw that there are reasons for that, both internal and external.

The external reason is the competitiveness of the particular product, the internal is the price band that you have, and your ability to change it. On external, there is not much we can do about, except trying to avoid selling products that are also sold cheaper by much stronger competitors.

There is not much sense in trying to compete in selling mass products with such giants as Tesco, Amazon, or Game. You need to find a niche, find products where you can be competitive. There are such products, they do exist. When you receive a stock list from a distributor with thousands of items every day, after making careful analysis, you can choose a few items that can make a profit for you after reselling.

The suppliers stock list change every day, because products sell out and more products arrive, and the list of products that you buy from a particular supplier changes too. And here we can repeat the thought that we have made in Chapter 1, that you need to deal with more than supplier. If each of the suppliers can offer you even a few products which are right for you, those that you can resell profitably, then several of such suppliers can provide you with some variety in your stock list.

Enough about prices, in the next chapter we will discuss how to increase your volumes, build good relationship with your supplier, and develop further your account.

Chapter 4. New Releases vs. Back Catalogue Games

Concentrating on Back Catalogue Items, Rather than New Releases

There are over 5000 line items of video games offered on the market at any given time. That's a large number and obviously most of suppliers usually have significantly less variety of items in their stock. Large wholesale distributors with international coverage may want to have many of the available titles in their stock, including both new releases and back catalogue items that released some time ago. Smaller traders may not be able to keep massive stocks and have to choose what items they want to buy to keep in their stock. Having limited resources, smaller traders need to carefully decide what items to spend on their money to buy, so that they can resell them quickly and with higher margins.

Selling quickly and with higher margins, these are the key criteria really. Every buying decision should be based around that objective, invest in stock that turns over quickly and brings higher profit. The question is what items in the whole variety of video games can help to provide quick turn around and high margins. With all the large and small differences between various titles, including the quality of games, the platforms, the genres, and many other characteristics of games, all the games can be divided into two major categories, which make them significantly different in the way they are traded. These are new releases and back catalogue items.

New Releases

Throughout year many new releases arrive, with majority of them releasing during Autumn season. New releases can be either completely new titles or a newer versions of already existing franchises, for example FIFA, Call of Duty, Grand Theft Auto, etc. New releases are mostly sold on pre-orders, before the game is even printed and distributed. This includes both wholesale pre-orders by resellers, and retail pre-orders by end users.

At first it seems to be attractive to sell out all the stock even before getting it. New releases are more popular and demanded, especially triple-A titles, and it seems they could sell a lot. There are many caveats though when trading new releases compared with back catalogue.

1. New releases loose their price very quickly

After new release arrives in the market, within couple of weeks its price may start decreasing. Some titles loose their price quite quickly some may keep the price for several more weeks, depending on the supply, if it is scarce the price may keep a little longer, although it will eventually go down anyway.

2. Trading new release is very competitive.

The fact is that it seems so good to sell new releases make selling them very competitive, when a new release comes out almost every supplier offers it. Imagine a single item offered by almost all suppliers. This pushes the prices and consequently the margins down. Some suppliers engage in price battles with each other to be able to offer a better deal and win a sale.

In addition, because new releases loose their prices quickly, traders try to sell their new released stock as quickly as possible. If they are not quick enough, the market price may fall below their buying price and they will incur loss.

Because traders try to get rid of their new release stock quickly, this pushes the prices for them even further down. Many traders have quite anxious times before they sell their initial stock that has been purchased with high price, as it is quite easy to incur loss if anything goes wrong at this stage.

3. Traders must be able to make good forecast of future demand

Many new releases are sold on pre-orders. Traders buy them from their suppliers on pre-orders too. Many suppliers sell out all their stock on pre-orders even before the release date. For that reason if a trader pre-orders less quantity that he/she can resell, then after selling out, they might not be able to increase their pre-order as by that time their supplier may be sold out too. In this case the trader will have to stop selling this item anymore and will lose potential sales.

On the other hand, if the trader pre-orders too many, he/she might not be able to sell all the stock and will still have the stock in hand by the time it starts losing its price. In that case trader will incur loss because they may have to sell the remaining stock with lower margin or even below the cost just to get rid of it. For this reason it is important to be able to accurately estimate correct quantities of stock that will be needed, and it's quite difficult.

4. Logistics of new releases is significantly more complicated

The fact that new releases are mostly sold on pre-orders before the stock is available, creates additional chances for something in the process to go wrong. Buyers and sellers agree on the price and the quantity of the pre-order, with sellers selling stock that is not even in their warehouse yet, meaning that it is still outside of their control.

Many things can go wrong, for example sellers supplier (the publisher or a distributor) may delay sending the stock to them. Or they may send in time, but the freight forwarder that delivers the stock can delay the shipment.

After the stock arrives, the warehouse is under a lot of stress to quickly accept the stock and then ship all the pre-orders to customers. The freight forwarder that delivers to the customers may become a cause of additional delay, and so on.

Everything is under extreme rush and stress. Publishers usually ship new release stock few days before the release date, and the stock should go through the whole distribution chain, with wholesalers and retailers, and needs to get delivered to stores and put on the shelves before the release date. The maximum urgency and stress on the logistics make more possibilities for mistakes.

All these issues make selling new releases rather difficult and stressful job.

Back Catalogue

Unlike new releases, back catalogue items are mostly free from these problems. Catalogue items have already lost their prices time ago. Further reduction in their price is much slower and less dramatic. Traders can keep back catalogue items in their stock quite long time without any danger of price loss, and can be more relaxed when selling them. There is much more variety of catalogue items in market than new releases, and selling them is not as competitive as new releases, which are only a few dozen titles per year, compared with many thousands of catalog titles. When buying catalogue items, unlike new releases, there is no need to think hard and forecast the future demand and necessary quantities, traders can buy exactly as many items as necessary now. The logistics is significantly easier too, as there is usually no much stress and urgency compared with the rush of trying to get new releases on the shelves in time.

Conclusion

Dealing with new releases is stressful and provides little to no profit. So, why bother doing them at all then? The answer is because the customers demand them, and suppliers must be able to satisfy this demand, so that their customers do not have to turn to other suppliers for these items. Plus, after doing new releases for some time, and after gaining some valuable experience, and learning how to accurately estimate the demand, and after finding a range of sound and reliable suppliers who offer competitive prices, and after building a reliable logistics and distribution chain, over the time, it is possible for a trader to become profitable on new releases and start making a good profit on them too. Though the major money still remains to be earned on back catalogue items.

Chapter 5. Selling Video Games to Wholesalers and Retailers

In the previous chapters we have looked at how to buy video games from wholesalers. This included finding proper wholesalers, opening accounts with them, and then trying to get better prices from them.

What if we want not only to buy from wholesalers but also to sell to them?

The reason you, as a game business, buy games is to resell them and make profit. You may sell games to the end users, i.e. gamers, or if you are a wholesale video game trader, once you buy stock , you sell it to other traders. As a wholesaler you sell your stock to other game companies, either to retailers or to other wholesalers. This is a so called business-to-business (B2B) trade.

The idea of selling to wholesalers may seem a bit challenging for a small company which doesn't turn over much stock. But it is quite realistic, even for a small company, to be able to sell to other game companies, retailers and wholesalers. In fact significant number of small companies manage to sell to larger wholesalers every now and then. Some of small wholesalers sell to large companies even on permanent basis.

In reality it is not that difficult as it may seem. Significant part of the success is in your buying ability, to find and stock products with good demand and for good prices. If you get good stock with relevant prices, selling it becomes more of a technique. Let's have a look at the major components necessary for successful selling.

Stock List

First of all you need to have a stock list, which accurately reflects what items you have in stock, in what quantities, and their current prices. You have to send your stock list to your customers every day, preferably in the morning, so that they can send you their orders during the day.

The stock list needs to be updated every day, in order to reflect any changes that may have happened in the previous day after the previous stock list was sent out. This includes new arrivals of stock, changes in the quantities of the existing stock due to some stock being sold, with some of the items may be even getting out of stock. The changes in the stock list would also reflect any changes in the prices that you may be willing to make.

The easiest and most convenient is to make a stock list in an Excel sheet. A sample for Excel stock list is shown below.

	A	B	C	D	E	F
1	SKU	Item	Type	Stock	Price	Barcode
2	68791	Call of Duty: Black Ops 4 (PS4)	PS4	123	45	5030917239205
3	12345	FIFA 19 (PS4)	PS4	27	42	5030945121916
4						
5						

As you can see it's quite simple. The first column is SKU (Stock Keeping Unit), an ID number that you give your products for easy reference.

The second column is item name including the platform. The third is the type, i.e. the game platform.

The fourth column shows the quantity of the stock available. Note that this number is not necessarily the quantity of the item that you keep in the warehouse, if some of the stock is already reserved, then less quantity is available for sale. For example, if you have 24 pcs of GTA 5 (PS4) in your warehouse but 22 pcs are already reserved by your customers, then your stock list should show only 2pcs in stock, because only 2 pcs are available for sale. The rest is already sold even though they are still physically in your warehouse. The stock list needs to indicate the available quantity not the total physical quantity stored.

The fifth column indicates the wholesale price. You may remember from the previous chapters that wholesale prices may have banding. If you would like to have price banding for your customers, then you will need to prepare several versions of stock lists, one for each banding, every day.

If you sell in more than one country, you may have to deal with multiple currencies. You can include prices in several currencies in the same stock list. For example in the sample above, the next column to the Price USD may include prices in other currency, for example in GBP, or Euro. For simplicity we have not included these additional columns above, but you can make your stock list with multiple currencies. USD, GBP, and Euro are usually enough to cover most of the countries.

Of course your stock list will probably include more items than the two items in the example above, however the number of columns will probably be similar. You may want to add more columns with information that may be useful for your customers, for example another extra column may include languages of the game if necessary, and any other.

Daily Emails

Stock lists should be sent to your customers by email every day. The Excel files can be attached to emails. In addition some product highlights may be added to the body of the email. For example some interesting arrivals, or items with price reduction, or some bundles including few games with special price can be included in the email body. Pictures of the products may also be included in the email body for better visual reference.

In order to make sending emails easier, you may include different customers in different groups. For example you can group customers by price band. It is quite easy to organize in Microsoft Outlook if you use Windows or iOS. Some other mail programs have grouping feature too.

For example if there are four price bands, you may group your customers in four groups based on their price band, open four groups in Outlook and prepare four excel files of stock lists with different price band each. Then you attach each stock list in a separate email and send corresponding emails to each of the groups. In this way, you make sure that each customer receives stock list with their appropriate price band.

Your daily emails are very convenient also for your customers to send you orders. They can just reply to your daily email and include their order.

It is very important to send daily emails every day. That's also a way to remind about yourselves to your customers. As much as it may seem outdated, the email marketing still remains one of the most effective ways of direct marketing. If you don't email your customers regularly, they will just forget about you, whereas your competitor, who emails them regularly, will get orders.

Important: Remember to include your customers email addressed to the 'Bcc' field when you send them mass emails, not in 'To' field, otherwise they will be able to see each other names and email addresses. This will create two major problems. First you would violate their privacy by publicly showing their addresses to others. Second, more importantly, you don't want your competitors and your customers to learn about each other, otherwise they may start trading directly, eliminating you from the middle.

Phone Calls

Phone is used for selling to different extend in different countries. It is very common to use phone calls for trading in English-speaking countries. Moreover, a new buyer is unlikely to buy proper quantities from you before speaking to you in person, at least once. Some buyers would speak to you in the beginning to get acquainted, some buyers may prefer to always make buying by phone. It seems a bit strange in our time, when the communication means are so developed and diverse. In addition to emails, which seem more convenient for sending orders than phone, many websites have online ordering forms. But with all these, phone communication still remains one of the most common and effective, if not the most effective way of communication in trade.

Building your sales

Selling wholesale video games is business-to-business trade, with a limited number of business customers, who periodically come back to the seller for buying more. This makes it very important to keep your customers happy. Of course, keeping customers happy is important also in retail trade when selling to numerous customers. But in wholesale trade where you may have only a handful of customers, making your customers happy becomes of vital importance.

Many business buyers purchase video games on daily basis, to keep their stock levels. Such customers can buy a lot, and can bring a lot of business to you company. For this to happen, it is important to build good relationship with your customers.

Building relationship with customers is a long process requiring significant effort from your part. It is necessary to understand your customers, and what makes them buy from you, and what you, as a seller, can do so that they continue buying or buy even more.

One thing to always keep in mind is that buyers do not look for the cheapest price, they look for the best value. For example, if a supplier offers the cheapest prices but is not reliable, i.e., may send a shipment late or not send at all, then buyers most probably would prefer not to buy from such a supplier even though they are the cheapest. On the other hand, if you provide the best quality service, but are insanely expensive, then the buyer will not be able to make a profit, and can't buy, no matter how wonderfully pleasant it is to buy from you.

The buyers are looking for a good balance of price and quality, i.e. the best value for their money. If a buyer starts periodically buying from you, with the time the value may increases, because with the time, you, as the seller, learn the buyers preferences better, and are able to provide even better service and better value.

Buyers are humans like all of us, they would like to save not only their money but also to save their time and their effort. Which means that if they find a supplier who is more or less good for them, they would stick to that supplier. Until, of course, that supplier starts making mistakes, provide worse service, increases prices unreasonably, etc. In other words if the supplier loses value for the buyer. If another supplier can provide better value, the buyer would probably buy from them instead.

It is important to try to learn what your customer needs and to memorize it. You might want even to write down in a notebook, for some customers, in order to remember what they are looking for. This may include, for example, some games that they would like that are not in stock at the moment. Later, when that game arrives and appears in your stock, it is a good reason to give your customer a phone call and say, "Hey, remember, you were asking about this game the other day? We got that in stock now! Would you like to order it?"

This gives two major benefits. First of all you will get a sale, because the customer most probably would order that game since you bothered to call him specifically for that. Not only that but more importantly, the customer would be impressed and will appreciate your call and the fact that you remembered what he wanted and came back to him. That's a little trick to gain a good credit, and another block in building good relationship with your customer.

Building relationship with the customer happens on various levels, and might also include personal level. Buyers are people and of course they appreciate good, friendly treatment, and might want to engage in some small talk about the weather or the holiday they had recently been, before they start making an order. Others may be more to the point and prefer not to spend time on unnecessary conversations.

Constant search for new customers

Looking for customers is a permanent process. Even the most successful sales people who have large customer base of efficient buyers, never stop looking for new customers. In fact, it's because they always spend some time on daily basis for looking for new customers, they are successful and have a good quality customer base. And they constantly improve it. This has been already indicated in Chapter 2, for the case of buyers, that the search for suppliers is an ongoing process. Obviously the same applies for the customers. Search for customers may take significant portion of time during the day, especially at low season.

Improving the quality of the customers' list

Every seller tries to increase their customer base in order to increase sales. There is however a limit of how many accounts can be effectively managed by a single sales person. Because of this, sales reach certain level and flat out, i.e. cannot be increased any more. They way to overcome this is to improve the quality of the customer base. This is achieved by getting rid of inefficient customers, and acquiring new, better customers. Inefficient customers are those who take a lot of time from sales person but do not buy much. By substituting less efficient customers the sales person can increase sales.

Less buying customers can be for example passed to other sales people if a seller works in a team, for example in the sales team of a wholesale distributor. There might be other sales people who might be glad to get any, even not very efficient customers, due to the fact that they might be new employees who are still building their customer base, are not very experienced, or not very skilled in finding new customers. By substituting customers a successful sales person can further increase sales.

Increasing Average order

Sales person should also try to eventually increase the order amount by each of their accounts. Buyers normally should be well informed about the product, but in reality it's not always the case. During sales if seller provides valuable information, it can bring additional sales. For example, seller can proactively offer best-selling items that currently sell very well. It is good to be able to group products by certain criteria. For example if the seller notices that a buyer purchases games with low age limit, i.e. for children, the seller may offer other similar games for children, and there is a good chance that the buyer may want to purchase them too. Another grouping may be sports games, car racing titles, or other.

Another big group or products are non-game items, such as accessories, merchandise, figurines, etc. Many buyers don't even realise the potential off such items. Good salesman can educate buyers of possibilities of previously omitted products.

Very good potential in increasing sales is to bundle different items. This requires good product knowledge.

It's good if the items are related but it is not always a requirement. For example back catalog non-expensive items may be bundled into 2 – 3 game offers with attractive prices. If the buyer buys them, they can later use the same bundles for reselling to their customers, for example the retail customers. Games may be also bundles with accessories, for example controllers. Sometimes the opposite also happens, bundles get unbundled, for example console plus game bundles may be unbundled and sold separately. A lot of these combinations on bundling/unbundling emerge during conversations with the buyer. By discussing various options, seller can work out some offers that will be accepted by the buyer. That is why speaking by phone to the customers is so important. If the communication between buyer and seller was carried only by email, some options may never get even mentioned and realized.

Seasonality and Planning the Year

Video game trade has high seasonality. The majority of trade happens during couple of months before Christmas. Months of October, November, and first-half of December provide majority of sales throughout the year. Major triple-A releases are also scheduled around the same time. Things become more quiet on second half of December till mid-January. The second half of January and February become active again and may provide some good sales. Things become really quiet starting from March – April and onward. Late Spring and especially Summer are the low sales seasons. Sales eventually pick up again starting from September.

This affects on how you should schedule your work throughout the year. In the peak-season, most of the time is spent on getting orders and processing them, i.e. the account management. There is no much time left on anything else in that period. This is of course if you have good customer base.

Starting from March, there are not too many orders, and the majority of time during the day should be spent on acquiring new customers. Researching, sending emails, speaking with potential customers, with the objective of gaining new accounts, which will provide you with good sales at the peak-season. During the low season that's also the time you want to take your annual leave and settle any other non-work related matters.

Good practice, in any season, is to divide the day on both acquiring new business and managing existing accounts. The percentage of the time spent on each of these activities would vary depending on the season, as described above.

Your daily routine as a sales person will then include all of these activities: preparing the stock lists for each price band, sending out emails with the stock lists, processing the orders that arrived by email overnight and sending them to the accounting and the warehouse, plus spending some time also to new business development, i.e., finding new customers. This list includes the minimum that any sales people should do at work every day in order to be successful.

Conclusion

To summarise, good selling practice should include:

- Keep stock lists, always know what you have in stock so that you know what you can sell.
- Send emails with your stock lists to all your customers every day.

- Use phone for calling your customers as much as you can. Good practice is to call each customer at least monthly. If possible even weekly.
- Build good relationship with customers. Show individual approach. Remember what they are looking for and proactively offer it. Try to provide good value to your customers.
- Constantly search for new customers and improve your customer base, i.e. substitute low sales customers with new, higher sales ones.
- Gradually increase average order of each of your customers. Try to bundle products to make them more attractive for your customer.
- Keep in mind the high seasonality of video game sales, and plan your year accordingly.

Chapter 6. What are Game Codes, CD Keys, Digital Distribution…

Game Codes, CD Keys, Digital Distribution… these terms are becoming increasingly common and usable in PC and video game business. Instead of selling PC games on a media like DVD disk, more and more of them are distributed digitally through Internet.

PC games are recorded on CDs (or DVDs), and in order to prevent unauthorized copying and distribution, each copy of a game is supplied with a unique identification number, a so called "CD key". CD keys consist of a combination of 13, 15, 18, or 25 letters and numbers, which are usually printed on a sticker inside a game case or on the quick reference card.

PC games may be distributed online, customers can download them from a website, and they also need to be supplied with unique game keys in order to activate their copy. It makes distribution quite easy, as allows to avoid logistics, picking, packing, and shipping. It also allows to instantly deliver purchases, which makes it more convenient for the end users.

The business of digital distribution is rapidly growing, and more and more companies offer game activation keys for a wide range of computer games. The largest independent digital distributor is Steam. Some publishers have their specialized online distributions for selling their games, for example Sony has PlayStation Store, Electronic Art's online store is called Origin, Ubisoft's store is Uplay, Blizzard's site is Battle.net, etc. Major online retailers, which traditionally sell boxed products, such as Amazon, Game, also sell more and more digital downloads of game.

Independent re-sellers have good opportunity to make business on digital distribution. Many suppliers currently obtain game keys for reselling from boxed products. Games get opened and cd keys get scanned and sold through websites. Games can be downloaded for example from Steam, if they are on Steam, and using these game keys can be activated on user's computers. This practice, although being legitimate, is not encouraged by game publishers. Publishers prefer boxed PC games sold as boxed, not opened and game key sold separately. If a company would like to become a digital distributor, they should contact game publishers and apply to become their authorized digital distributor, if successful, they will get CD keys digitally from publishers.

Another major issue for game companies selling CD keys online is the VAT issue, especially in European countries. Since games are downloaded through Internet, there is no accurate indication and control on where it has been downloaded and hence where the actual sale has happened. This brings an ambiguity in VAT reporting. Since this is quite new sector, the tax offices of many countries are still working on developing proper reporting and monitoring procedures, and in this transition period many companies may still find it difficult to prove all their sales and VAT waiver claims.

One way or another, whether the game keys are obtained from boxed products or whether they are received in digital form from publishers, selling games online in digital form is a fast growing sector, and an increasing number of companies get involved. You can find list of major digital distributors and retailers of games in our database.

Chapter 7. Dropshipping

What is Dropshipping

Dropshipping is retailing without necessity to keep stock. Instead, your wholesale supplier sends the stock directly to your customer. You (reseller) forward your customer's order and the shipment details to your supplier (dropshipper), and they ship the goods on your behalf directly to your customer. Customers are not aware that the goods are drop shipped, as so called "private label shipping" allows shipping from your wholesaler with a return address and invoice customized to your store.

Benefits of Dropshipping

1. Low Start-up costs

If you trade under dropshipping model, you don't need to spend cash on buying initial stock, renting a warehouse space, and organizing the logistics, including processing orders, picking and packing the stock, labelling and shipping. This allows to save significant initial investment and allows easy entry for start-ups.

2. Simplified Operations

Reseller that uses dropshipping does not need to have full functionality of a traditional retailer, it may cut storing, logistics, handling shipments, and deliveries. In a traditional store these functions require having relevant facilities, such as storage, order picking and sorting area, as well as having the personnel who performs these functions.

Another major area that reseller may cut is the buyers function. Buying is one of the most difficult functions in trade. It requires significant experience from the buyer and a deep market knowledge. Wrongly purchased stock may stay unsold or may sell very slowly, creating losses, wasted working capital, and occupy space in the warehouse. For this reason, buyer's job is usually quite high profile and is associated with risks, and eliminating this function significantly simplifies trading operations. In case of dropshipping, there is no buying of stock on a regular basis, a trader just enters in an agreement with a dropshipper and just offers dropshipper's stock, and is basically limited by what the dropshipper can offer. A trader may have more than one dropshipper and thus expand its range of products, though this might be associated with additional cost, as many dropshippers, in addition to cost of products, may also charge an additional fixed subscription fees.

3. Global scale

Your dropshipper need to be local to your customers but you don't have to. You can operate your store from anywhere as long as your dropshipper is able to fulfil them locally. For each geographical region that you would like to operate you may have a local dropshipper and cover large and distant locations. Isn't this consistent with a dream of many, laying down on a sunny beach, with a nice cocktail, and your laptop, and orchestrate your online business through Internet, a couple of hours per day, while dropshippers do the rest for you.

By now you have probably came to understand that this is becoming too good to be true, didn't you? Ok, let's have a look at some potential problems.

Problems of Dropshipping

1. Stock availability issues

When you sell goods from your own stock, you can reliably fulfil your orders and there are rarely any issues with availability of stock since you know what you have and you only sell what you have. If you sell dropshippers stock, quite often you can't see their stock list live. In most cases, you get their stock list in the morning and can't see changes that happen during a day, for example some items may get sold out, and if you are not aware and continue selling, this will create problem and dissatisfaction from your customers if after you receive an order and payment, your dropshipper is not able to deliver the order since the stock is already sold out. Some more traditional retailers who stock goods in their warehouses, still may also apply "get order then get stock" scheme for some less demanded items. But there is a difference as if after getting an order they find that one of the suppliers is out of stock for that item, they may quickly find the item with another supplier. With dropshipper scheme there is much less flexibility in that.

2. Control and Responsibility

A complicated mechanism breaks down more frequently than a simpler one. Adding a third party to fulfil your orders increases chances of fulfilment errors, mistakes, and logistical problems. Plus there is an issue of responsibility, who is responsible for customer returns? There is a significant number of returns in video games industry, justified and unjustified, most dropshippers would not deal with it, so the reseller has to.

3. Marketing and Promotion

Having an online store is not enough for selling, your store should be visible to your customers otherwise they won't find you. One of the major things you have to ensure in your marketing and promotion efforts, that your site is well received and visible by major search engines. Google, which is the major search engine, does not quite favour multiple listings from the same vendor. Keep in mind, you will be not the only reseller of a given dropshipper, there might be dozens, if not hundreds, of resellers who will be advertising products of the same supplier on their sites. If you use the dropshipper's product listings, in online terms your website essentially becomes an affiliate of the dropshipper, and you must know that Google does not like affiliated websites.

The reason is because when somebody searches Google for a particular product, the search engine tries to give a variety of most relevant results. If the results include you, and many other resellers of the same dropshipper, that would not be a variety it would essentially be the same product of the same dropshipper, advertised by various resellers. To avoid this, Google filters down most of resellers from its results, leaving may be one, or even sometimes none of the same supplier.

You can also resell on Ebay and Amazon, but you will have to compete on price with traditional retailers who stock their goods are able to offer less price and better reliability.

4. Higher costs lead to higher prices

Dropshippers charge extra margin compared with traditional wholesale distributors. This margin includes extra cost for logistics and handling, also, since with dropshipper you place a number of small orders rather than one big order, you get higher prices for each product. As a result it becomes very difficult, if at all possible to compete with retailers who buy large quantities from traditional wholesalers. For example, you got a price of 62 USD including VAT for a recently released PS4 game (Fifa or Call of Duty, etc), and would like to sell it in Europe. The dropshipper charges you extra 4.67 USD for P&P, which brings the price to 66.67 USD. A quick glance at amazon.co.uk, or amazon.de indicates that the same game is sold for only 60 USD including VAT, and your price is simply not competitive.

Conclusion

It seems easy on the first glance but it isn't. In fact, opening an online store solely for reselling dropshippers products gives little chance to be successful, you may just loose time and money. It makes more sense to add reselling dropshippers' product to an already existing successful operation. For example if you have a successful blog about video games, with high traffic visiting your site and some active and loyal visitors, you may try to monetize it by offering some products on your site, and to avoid dealing with fulfillment of orders, you may partner with a dropshipper. Google will look at it much more favorably, and may still love your site if it offers good value, such as interesting articles, product reviews, engaging customers, who participate, leave comments, etc.

Though if you have a good, actively visited website, you may want also to consider other ways of monetisation, such as affiliate programs, for example, Amazon's Affiliate Program allows listing of its products on your site and each time someone buys anything you get a small commission. There are many other ways to monetize a successful website, and dropshipping arrangement is one of them. You may want to do some comparison of available options, may be experiment with some suppliers and affiliate programs to find the optimal option for your case.

Otherwise, if you like to more concentrate on trade, it's probably a good idea to follow a traditional trading model, i.e. deal with traditional wholesale distributors, buy stock from them on a regular basis, store it in your warehouse, and sell items that you have in stock.

Chapter 8. **Trading with Amazon**

Amazon is the world's largest online retailer. In addition to its main website at amazon.com and its distribution centre in the United States, it also has websites and distribution centres in many other countries, including United Kingdom, France, Germany, Italy, Spain, Canada, Australia, Brazil, Japan, China, India and Mexico. Trading with amazon may provide huge potential for any company trading video games, consoles, electronics, DVD's, etc.

There are two ways to trade with Amazon.

1. Sell <u>on</u> Amazon, Sellers account, retail trade

2. Sell <u>to</u> Amazon, Vendor account, wholesale trade

1. Selling on Amazon, Sellers account, retail trade.

In addition to selling directly to end customers, Amazon also provides a platform for other traders to sell on its website. It is called Amazon Marketplace. This gives Amazon's customers a choice to buy an item either directly from Amazon, using so called "Buy Box", or from other sellers, in "More Buying Choices" box. For becoming a seller on Amazon, a company needs to create a Seller account at https://services.amazon.com/content/sell-on-amazon.htm/.

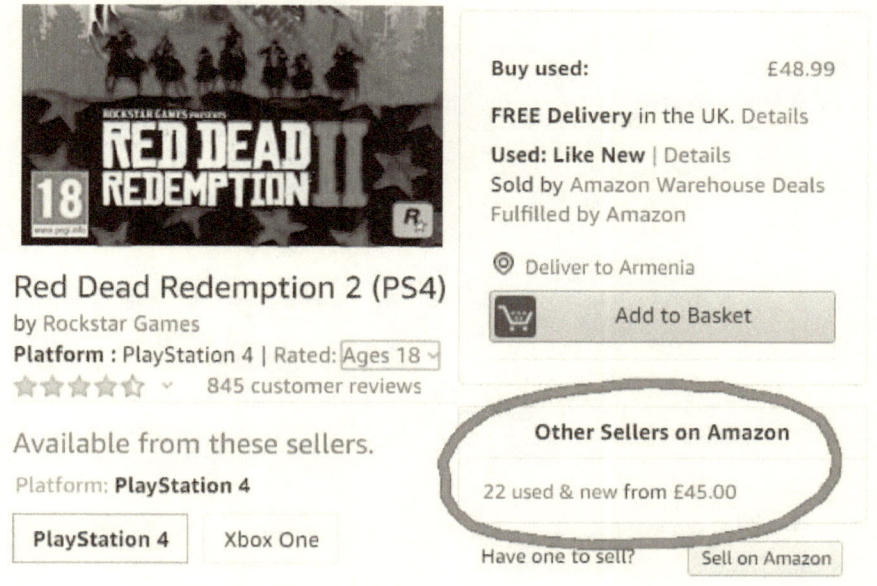

Depending on volumes that the company is planning to sell, it may chose to register either as professional or individual.

Selling on Amazon provides access to millions of Amazon's customers. Amazon provides images and descriptions for sold items on its site, plus, once an order is made, Amazon also handles the payments for the sellers. What sellers have to do is only to deliver the sold items to the end customers.

£49.99 ✓prime & Eligible for FREE UK Delivery. Details	New	amazon.co.uk	• Delivery rates and return policy.	Add to B
£49.99 + £2.03 Delivery	New	AndyWills ☆☆☆☆☆ 0% positive over the past 12 months. (1 total ratings)	• Dispatched from United Kingdom. • Delivery rates and return policy.	Add to B
£49.99 + £2.03 Delivery	New	Offer-Games ☆☆☆☆☆ 67% positive over the past 12 months. (6 total ratings)	• Dispatched from United Kingdom. • Delivery rates and return policy.	Add to B
£47.99 + £4.06 Delivery	New	Super Duper ☆☆☆☆☆ 98% positive over the past 12 months. (14,822 total ratings)	• Dispatched from United Kingdom. • Delivery rates and return policy.	Add to B
£52.90 + £1.95 Delivery	New	Warby 4 Games & Gifts ☆☆☆☆☆ 97% positive	• Dispatched from United Kingdom. • Delivery rates and return policy.	Add to B

There is a monthly fee plus commission for Sellers, depending on volume and country. Pro sellers pay monthly fee of $39.99 and can sell unlimited amount of items, and individual sellers do not have to pay any monthly amount but have to pay $0.99 on each sold item. A list of applicable fees can be found on Sellers account page.

An additional service called "Fulfilled by Amazon" (FBA) is available for Sellers, who would like Amazon to also do delivery for them. Sellers ship their items to Amazon's warehouse, where they get stored, and after making a sale, the delivery is made from Amazon's distribution centre. There is an extra charge for the FBA service.

2. Selling to Amazon. Vendor account, wholesale.

Amazon sells huge volumes across many product lines. In order to sell huge quantities, Amazon needs to buy huge quantities from its suppliers. It sources goods from many vendors. Amazon buys not only directly from publishers and manufacturers but also from third party independent suppliers. Becoming a vendor means that your products appear in so called Amazon's "Buy Box", i.e, when customers click on "Buy" to buy from Amazon, they are essentially buying from Amazon's vendor. In theory becoming a vendor means much greater volumes of sale, though there are also drawbacks.

Two major drawbacks include (1) Amazon sets retail sale prices itself and vendor has no control over it, unlike Seller account holders; (2) Amazon takes a major, 55% commission for each vendor sale, compared to only 5 – 20% for sellers accounts. Major advantage is that most Amazon website users prefer to buy directly from Amazon rather than other sellers, and this provides significantly larger sales for vendors.

Becoming a seller to Amazon is by invitation only. Amazon sends invitations together with application forms. In order to become a vendor and sell wholesale to Amazon, companies need to visit Amazon's Vendor Central portal at https://vendorcentral.amazon.com/gp/vendor/ and request a new account through special form at https://vendorcentral.amazon.com/hz/vendor/public/contact page.

After receiving your request, Amazon would evaluate it, and if it finds your company eligible as potential vendor, an account manager from Amazon would contact you to discuss your application further and will send you an electronic invitation code for making an application. Sometimes Amazon may itself encourage most active Seller account holders to shift to a vendor account. Companies need to make careful calculation before they decide if they want to have a seller account or a vendor account.

Selling on Amazon may be quite profitable. Companies that diversify their customer portfolio should definitely consider also Amazon platform. Amazon continues expanding and is aiming to increase its market share even more in future. It has been very successful so far, and there is no reason to assume that this will not continue at least in near future. Traders of all size can benefit, they should keep Amazon in mind as one of the biggest players in the market and try to think of ways to use their position and trade with them, rather than compete with them.

www.ingramcontent.com/pod-product-compliance
Lightning Source LLC
Chambersburg PA
CBHW020614220526
45463CB00006B/2589